Beyond Solitude

(Alone no More)

P K Singh

ALSO, BY P K SINGH

<u>Books</u>

*CRACKING SAFETY AND HSE JOB INTERVIEW **

<u>(Includes 200+ important Questions and Answers)</u>

INTERVIEWER'S CHOICEST QUESTIONS

(Covers difficult Interview Questions and Answers

PROCESS SAFETY ENGINEER *

INTERVIEW GUIDE

FIRE WATCH, SAFETY FOREMAN, RIGGER AND
OPERATOR INTERVIEW GUIDE *

THE PETROLEUM INDUSTRY

CRUDE OIL EXPLORATION & REFINING

*Available from Amazon

Please visit:

<u>https://www.amazon.com/author/pksingh</u>

DEDICATION

To My Dearest Wife, Son, And Daughter,

This book is a testament to the love and support that each of you has brought into my life.

To my wife, your unwavering encouragement and understanding have been the cornerstone of my journey. Your love is the inspiration behind every word written here.

To my son, watching you grow into the incredible person you are fills my heart with pride. May the stories within these pages be a source of guidance and inspiration as you navigate the path ahead, knowing that you carry the strength and wisdom within you to overcome any challenge.

To my daughter, your grace, intelligence, and warmth bring joy to my days. May this book serve as a reminder of the boundless possibilities that await you and the love that surrounds you at every step of your journey.

Together, you form the tapestry of my life, and this book is a small reflection of the gratitude and love I feel for each of you. Thank you for being my pillars of strength, my sources of joy, and my greatest blessings.

With all my love,

P K Singh

Table of Contents

ACKNOWLEDGMENTS

As I pen down these words on loneliness, I am reminded that no creative endeavor is solitary. This exploration into the depths of solitude has been a collective effort, and I am grateful for the support and inspiration that have surrounded me throughout this journey.

I extend my deepest gratitude to those who shared their personal stories of loneliness, vulnerability, and resilience. Your courage has added profound depth to the narrative, and I am humbled by your willingness to open your hearts.

To my friends and family, thank you for your patience, understanding, and unwavering support during the moments when I retreated into the solitude required for this work. Your belief in the importance of this exploration fueled my determination.

A special acknowledgment goes to Ms. Shibani, whose expertise and insights greatly enriched the content of this book. Your guidance was invaluable, and I am thankful for the collaborative spirit that defined my work.

I am indebted to the countless authors, thinkers, and researchers whose work on loneliness inspired me to lay a foundation for this book

Lastly, to the readers who embark on this journey with me, thank you for your curiosity and willingness to explore the complexities of loneliness. May these pages offer solace, understanding, and a shared sense of connection.

With sincere appreciation,

P K Singh

PREFACE

Loneliness is approaching epidemic proportions in our culture, as seen by soaring suicide rates and increased mental disease. More than ever, we need to find a way to connect. Loneliness is a sensation of separation or isolation; it is not always the same as being physically alone. This book is for individuals who suffer from loneliness that cannot be alleviated simply by being near other people. Their loneliness is a deeply established pattern that is both negative and painful; it is frequently driven by trauma, loss, addiction, grief, and a lack of self-esteem and uncertainty.

Anyone can suffer loneliness; it doesn't matter their age, background, or situation. In this book, we explore the ins and outs of loneliness, looking at its causes, effects, and—above all—offering workable solutions. It's possible to overcome loneliness; this book is meant to support you as you overcome obstacles and rediscover the happiness that comes from connecting with others.

Loneliness is a common thread in the fabric of human existence, appearing in the lives of several individuals. It's an experience that cuts over age, socioeconomic status, and situation. Our goal as we delve into this investigation of loneliness is to illuminate its intricacies and, above all, to serve as a guide for individuals traversing the very difficult terrain of isolation.

The paradox of loneliness endures in a society when technology seems to be connecting people more and more. Being lonely is more than just being alone; it's a complex emotional condition that can linger even in the middle of a busy street. Many people experience it, but they often find it difficult to express, and it's frequently accompanied by a feeling of shame or failure.

By allowing readers to face loneliness with empathy, understanding, and the awareness that they are not alone in their challenges, this book aims to dissolve such boundaries.

We will explore the emotional, social, and existential aspects of loneliness as we navigate these pages. We want to provide more than just insights—we want to be a lifeline for people who are looking for understanding and connection—through sympathetic experiences, useful tips, and the knowledge gained from individuals who have successfully weathered loneliness.

Being alone does not have to last a lifetime. These chapters explore the causes and effects of loneliness, but just as importantly, they offer advice on how to break free from its hold. We explore the significance of developing deep relationships, being self-aware, and how technology is influencing our social environment. The tales told in these pages are more than just stories; they are rays of hope that show the way to happiness and fellowship.

Let us keep in mind that vulnerability is a powerful force that unites us as human beings as we set out on this journey together rather than a sign of weakness. Understanding loneliness gives us the ability to change it, both as individuals and as a group that promotes empathy, compassion, and sincere connection.

May this book serve as a friend to those who find solace

in its pages, a guide to those in search of a connection, and a reminder that, within the pages of our own stories, we are all capable of rewriting the narrative of loneliness into one of resiliency, empathy, and the reassuring warmth of human connection.

- **P K Singh**

1: UNDERSTANDING LONELINESS

Being alone isn't the only thing that defines loneliness; it's a multifaceted feeling that can linger in even the busiest social situations. This chapter delves into the diverse aspects of loneliness, examining its meanings and comprehending the range of shapes it can become. We intend to give readers a solid basis on which to understand their own experiences with loneliness by illuminating the profundity of this feeling.

DEFINING LONELINESS

An emotional state known as loneliness is defined by a sensation of separation or loneliness from other people, which can leave one feeling empty and yearning for deep connections. It's important to distinguish between loneliness, which is frequently involuntary and linked to a lack of satisfying social interactions, and solitude, which is the conscious state of being alone.

TYPES OF LONELINESS

1. **Emotional Loneliness:** Even when surrounded by people, persons who experience emotional loneliness may not feel as intimate or connected to their relationships as they would like.

   When people feel extremely alone in their emotional lives, they are said to be emotionally lonely. They frequently feel alone or unsupported even while they are surrounded by people. These two instances demonstrate emotional loneliness:

The Masked Caregiver:

Picture a loving family member who is tasked with providing for the medical needs of a family member who has a chronic condition. Despite their rigorous performance of their caring responsibilities, they suffer a great deal emotionally. The caregiver could be reluctant to communicate their own worries, annoyances, or needs for assistance out of concern that showing their weakness might burden others. They sense emotional loneliness and want for recognition and understanding of their emotional challenges, even while they are physically there and actively involved in providing care.

The high-achieving student:

Imagine a high-achieving student who routinely achieves academic success in a classroom context. Despite appearing successful on the outside, this student can be emotionally alone. Although they may not be aware of the student's internal pressure and dread of failing, their friends, teachers, and families may praise their successes. Reluctant to acknowledge their fears and uncertainties, the student presents a front of assurance. Even though they are surrounded by intellectual triumphs, they feel lonely on an emotional level and long for someone to comprehend the emotional complexity that lies underlying their success.

2. **Social Loneliness:** Social loneliness is defined as the lack of a larger social network. It entails feeling excluded from social gatherings and activities.

People who experience a lack of connection and belonging in their social interactions or communities are said to be socially lonely. The following instances demonstrate social isolation:

A Brand-New Hire in a Big Company:

Consider a recently recruited worker who walks into a big company. Even with so many coworkers around them, the new hire could find it difficult to build genuine relationships. Cliques in the workplace may have developed over time and the culture may be well-established. Even though they participate in office activities and team gatherings, the new employee experiences social isolation. Their need for more meaningful relationships and a feeling of inclusion is strong, yet they struggle to fit in with the current social groups.

The Retiree in a New Neighborhood: Let us take into consideration a person who retired lately and relocated to a new neighborhood. Even though there are many community events and a welcoming area, the retiree can find it challenging to build strong relationships. Since many neighbors may have been friends for a long time, it may be difficult for the retiree to integrate into established social circles. The retiree feels socially isolated even though they attend neighborhood events and longs for closer relationships with neighbors who share their experiences and stage of life.

3. **Existential Loneliness:** A more profound and intellectual type of loneliness in which people struggle with a sense of meaninglessness in life.

A deep sense of isolation caused by a belief that life has no purpose or significance is known as existential loneliness

The Secular environment and the Spiritual Seeker: Consider a person with strong spiritual convictions living in a mostly secular environment. As they struggle with issues related to life's meaning, existence itself, and pursuing spiritual fulfillment, this individual could experience existential loneliness. Amidst a society that might not comprehend or concur with their spiritual beliefs, the individual seeking enlightenment feels incredibly alone on their existential quest.

The Elderly Scholar Considering the Purpose of Life: Imagine an old philosopher who has studied philosophy and pondered existential issues all of their lives. They could struggle with a feeling of existential loneliness as they get older. A perpetual seeker of meaning, the philosopher could feel lonely in his deep reflections, particularly if his opinions conflict with those of the majority. Seeking deep understanding at the expense of others who may not have similar philosophical questions might cause one to feel alone.

PERSONAL STORIES OF LONELINESS

Anis's Story: The Alone College Attendee

Bright college student Anis felt incredibly alone while being surrounded by a sea of people. She was surrounded by classmates, yet she found it difficult to build deep relationships. Her mental health started to suffer as a result of the seclusion, which had a negative impact on her general wellbeing and academic performance. The moving tale of Anis demonstrates how loneliness can have an impact on people even in vibrant social settings.

Jerome' Journey through Emotional Loneliness

Despite his professional accomplishments, Jerome, a successful man, experienced emotional loneliness. He found that he didn't have strong emotional ties to others because his rigorous work didn't provide much time for personal interactions. Though he was part of a large social circle, he longed for deeper connections. Jerome's narrative demonstrates how loneliness can materialize even in the face of achievement on the outside.

The purpose of sharing these tales is to educate readers about the universality of loneliness and the importance of admitting one's feelings of loneliness in order to find support and form deep connections.

Understanding loneliness entails figuring out its many facets, accepting its existence, and realizing that loneliness is a universal human experience. In order to help readers feel connected and realize they are not alone in their struggle, this chapter seeks to teach them the knowledge and awareness necessary to manage their own path through loneliness.

EMOTIONAL LONELINESS: **DIXY'S STORY**

A thriving social circle and a prosperous career surrounded Dixy, a dynamic and accomplished marketing executive. But below it all, she struggled with a severe case of emotional isolation.

Meetings, social gatherings, and networking activities occupied Dixy's weekdays. She appeared to have friends, a successful career, and a full social life on paper. But when the weekends drew near, a faint sense of emptiness emerged. Though there was humor and companionship, Dixy yearned for a more profound emotional bond that went beyond the surface level of social gatherings.

Dixy became aware that the majority of her encounters were transactional as she went about her everyday activities. Talks mostly focused on business, the news, and social graces; they hardly ever touched on vulnerabilities or inner thoughts. Despite being surrounded by people, she didn't have the kind of relationships that could offer understanding and emotional support.

The pivotal moment occurred amid a trying time at work. When a big project didn't proceed as expected, Dixy's supervisors gave her criticism. The customary get-togethers went on, but Dixy started to feel more and more alone. Her acquaintances were inadvertently preoccupied with their own lives and failed to see through her calm façade to the mental agony she was hiding.

Dixy desperately needed someone to confide in during this difficult time in her career about her worries, disappointments, and anxieties. Her emotional loneliness grew as a result of these deeper connections being absent. In spite of her success on the outside, she felt lost in a sea of acquaintances since she didn't have genuine emotional connections.

Dixy started by reflecting on herself before tackling her emotional loneliness. She actively sought out opportunities for deeper conversations since she understood the need for more meaningful connections. She gradually confided in close friends about her difficulties, enabling a more real emotional interchange.

Dixy learned via this process that emotional connection might be achieved through vulnerability. She encouraged others to share their own concerns and anxieties by doing so. Her relationships changed over time, and she developed a close-knit group of friends who gave her the emotional support she had been lacking.

Dixy's narrative emphasizes how critical it is to identify and treat emotional loneliness. It serves as a reminder that a person might have a terrible sense of loneliness even in the midst of a bustling social life if they lack strong emotional ties. This illustration prompts readers to examine their own emotional ties and the caliber of their relationships in negotiating the treacherous terrain of loneliness.

Example of Social Loneliness: Antony's Experience

Despite the continual presence of people, Antony, a software developer with a passion for code and technology, found himself enmeshed in a world that frequently seemed solitary. His experience is a moving illustration of social loneliness in which the number of social contacts did not always correspond to the quality of the relationship.

Antony was a devoted professional who worked long hours, immersed in creative ideas and complex code. Although his office was a hive of activity, with team meetings and joint projects going on all the time, Antony found it difficult to establish real relationships in this seemingly social environment. Lunch talks were all about business, and team building activities were fun, but they but they lacked the personal connection that Antony desired.

Weekends were the biggest difficulties for Antony. Even if his coworkers were participating in a variety of social events, Antony was frequently alone himself. He received invitations, but they were for social events or parties with big crowds that didn't offer the close relationships he was looking for. Antony had a strong sense of social isolation and a sensation of being outside of social circles even though he was surrounded by others.

Antony's realization that most of his social relationships were transactional and lacked the depth necessary to satisfy his yearning for meaningful connections marked a turning point in his life. Realizing the value of common interests outside of the workplace, Antony made the decision to look into local meatus pertaining to his interests in technology and coding.

Through these events, Antony was able to connect with people who shared his enthusiasm for technology. Conversations could go beyond the confines of work-related topics and become more casual and intimate. Antony made relationships with people who shared his interests and experiences gradually.

Because social loneliness is different from other types of loneliness, Antony's journey emphasizes that feeling like you belong is not a given just because you are surrounded by people. It emphasizes how crucial sincere contacts and common interests are in reducing social isolation. Readers are encouraged by this example to assess the quality of their social interactions, look for interests-related communities, and cultivate relationships that transcend beyond surface-level exchanges.

Example of Existential Loneliness: Reena's exploration

Reena, an artist who was deeply reflective, was struggling with existential loneliness, a distinct kind of loneliness. Her narrative reveals the intense isolation that can result from reflecting about life's meaning, purpose, and humanity.

Reena had a prosperous career as an artist, producing stunning pieces that touched many people. She frequently experienced a strong sensation of alienation despite being acknowledged by others. She had more queries than only those related to social activities and daily encounters. In the face of existential ambiguity, Reena found herself thinking about the size of the cosmos, the transient nature of life, and the search for meaningfulness.

Her art served as a vehicle for expressing these existential reflections and turned into a source of comfort as well as alienation. Reena found it difficult to connect with others who shared her introspective outlook on life, even when her creations struck a chord with those who valued the depth of her work. Friends and family conversations would frequently veer back into practical issues, which left Reena longing for dialogue that explored the deep issues that inspired her artistic expression.

In order to confront her existential loneliness, Reena carefully investigated philosophical and spiritual communities. She participated in talks, seminars, and retreats centered on life's most profound facets. Through these encounters, she came into contact with people who were dealing with comparable existential issues, which gave them a sense of connection that went beyond the commonplace.

Reena found a community that valued the intricacy and beauty of existential inquiry in these situations. The mutual reflection on life's riddles served as a link to deep and lasting relationships. Reena's narrative demonstrates how existential loneliness is a distinct and complex facet of the human experience that necessitates deliberate investigation and interaction with others who have a similar desire for a deeper meaning.

Readers are prompted by Reena's journey to consider their own existential questions, realizing that the search for purpose can be both a source of deep connection and isolation. It encourages people to look for groups and discussions that mirror their existential thoughts, creating a feeling of common purpose as they make their way through the vast and enigmatic terrain of existence.

THE IMPACT ON PHYSICAL AND MENTAL WELL-BEING

Being alone can have a serious negative influence on one's physical and mental health in addition to being an emotional burden. Chronic loneliness has been related in research to higher stress levels, anxiety, sadness, and even physical health problems including heart problems. The first step in addressing and lessening loneliness's negative impacts on our lives is realizing how severe it is.

Misunderstood as merely an emotional state, loneliness has a significant effect on one's physical and mental health. Humans are social animals with an inbuilt need for connection, and when this need is not satisfied, there can be consequences that go well beyond just emotional problems. In this investigation, we explore the complex ways that loneliness affects the body and the mind.

Physical Health Implications:

1. **Cardiovascular Health:** There is a correlation between loneliness and heightened cardiovascular risks. Research indicates that those who are lonely on a long-term basis can be more susceptible to cardiac problems due to greater blood pressure and stress levels. When loneliness results in persistently high levels of the stress hormone cortisol, this can exacerbate inflammation and increase the risk of heart disease. Further harming their physical health, lonely people may also take up unhealthy coping strategies like overeating or leading a sedentary lifestyle.

2. **Weakened Immune System:** Loneliness can affect our immune systems, which are what protect us from disease. Increased inflammation has been linked to chronic loneliness, and this could eventually impair the immune system and make people more susceptible to disease.

   An impaired immune response renders the body less capable of fighting off infections including bacteria, viruses, fungus, and other microbes. This disease is referred to as immunodeficiency or decreased immunity.

3. **Sleep Disturbances**: Feeling lonely can interfere with sleep cycles, making it harder to get to sleep and stay asleep. In consequence, insufficient sleep is linked to a number of health issues, such as weakened immune systems and decreased cognitive performance.

Loneliness can cause a variety of sleep problems and have a substantial impact on sleep patterns. There are several elements that affect the complex relationship between loneliness and sleep, including psychological and physiological ones. The following are some ways that loneliness may aggravate sleep issues:

Increased tension and Anxiety: Loneliness frequently coexists with increased tension and anxiety. The emotional pain associated with isolation can cause the release of stress hormones such as cortisol. Elevated cortisol levels, especially when chronic, can disrupt the natural sleep-wake cycle, making it difficult for people to fall or stay asleep.

Rumination and Overthinking: People who are lonely may ponder more and ruminate more than usual, especially at night. The stillness of the night might heighten emotions of loneliness and focus attention on unfavorable ideas and feelings. Rumination that never goes away might prevent people from relaxing their brains, which delay the start of sleep.

Modified Circadian Rhythms: The internal biological clocks that control the sleep-wake cycle can be thrown off balance by loneliness. A circadian rhythm that is out of line might be caused by alterations in daily schedules, inconsistent sleep patterns, or interruptions in social contacts. Difficulties going asleep at the intended bedtime or waking up at the proper hours in the morning could be caused by this misalignment.

Enhanced susceptibility to Insomnia: Research has connected loneliness to an increased susceptibility to insomnia. Difficulties getting to sleep, remaining asleep, or having restorative sleep are symptoms of insomnia. For those who experience it, sleeplessness can be a lifelong struggle because of the emotional anguish linked to loneliness, which can set off a vicious cycle of unfavorable ideas and actions.

Inadequate Sleep: A subjective sense of insufficient sleep might be influenced by loneliness. A person may feel restless or dissatisfied with their sleep even if they get enough sleep, which can make them feel exhausted and groggy during the day. This is because loneliness has an emotional price.

Improving the emotional impact of loneliness and addressing it can be essential to achieving better sleep. The influence of loneliness on sleep disturbances can be lessened by interventions that emphasize forming social relationships, taking part in joyful and fulfilling activities, and adopting good sleep hygiene habits. Professionals in the field of mental health can also offer helpful coping mechanisms for loneliness and ways to enhance general wellbeing, including sleep.

4. **Altered Hormonal Balance:** The control of stress hormones like cortisol can be impacted by loneliness. Extended exposure to high cortisol levels raises the chance of developing chronic diseases by exacerbating disorders like metabolic syndrome and insulin resistance.

The adrenal glands create the stress hormone cortisol, and the body naturally responds to stress by elevating this hormone. Long-term isolation or ongoing stress can raise cortisol levels, which can have detrimental effects on the immune system and metabolism, among other physiological functions.

Effect on Oxytocin Levels: Also known as the "bonding hormone" or the "love hormone," oxytocin is essential for social bonding and connection. Low oxytocin levels may be linked to loneliness. Decreased amounts of oxytocin can affect social interactions, emotional bonding, and trust, which may exacerbate feelings of loneliness and alienation.

Sleep Hormone Disturbances: The sleep-wake cycle and hormones involved in sleep regulation can be affected by loneliness. The hormone melatonin, which aids in sleep regulation, may be impacted by erratic sleeping habits linked to loneliness. The production of melatonin can be impacted by variations in the length and timing of sleep, which may make it harder to fall asleep or stick to a regular sleep schedule.

Effect on Ghrelin and Leptin: Hormones involved in hunger and metabolism, including ghrelin and leptin, may be impacted by loneliness. Leptin indicates fullness, whereas ghrelin is linked to appetite. The equilibrium between these hormones can be upset by altered social and emotional states, such as loneliness, which may lead to adjustments in hunger and eating habits.

Decreased Dopamine and Serotonin Activity: Studies have shown that depression and anxiety are associated with changes in the levels of neurotransmitters like dopamine and serotonin. These chemical messengers are essential for mood modulation even though they are not hormones in the conventional sense. Neurotransmitter activity alterations brought on by loneliness may exacerbate mood disorders and have an adverse effect on general wellbeing.

MENTAL HEALTH EFFECTS:

Depression and Anxiety: The development of anxiety and depressive illnesses is significantly influenced by loneliness. A chronic feeling of hopelessness, melancholy, and increased anxiety can be caused by the lack of significant social ties.

1. **Cognitive Decline:** Recent studies point to a possible connection between loneliness and cognitive aging. Alzheimer's disease and other types of dementia may be more common in people who experience prolonged loneliness.

2. **Negative Impact on Self-Esteem**: Feelings of rejection and isolation are frequently coupled with loneliness, which has a detrimental effect on self-esteem. Mental health issues may worsen if people absorb the idea that they are unworthy of respect or connection.

3. **Increased Stress Levels**: Stress hormone levels rise as a result of loneliness triggering the body's stress reaction. Prolonged stress exposure has been linked to a number of mental health problems, such as increased anxiety, impatience, and trouble controlling one's emotions.

The Bidirectional Relationship:

There is a reciprocal relationship between loneliness and mental and physical health. Although loneliness can aggravate pre-existing health conditions, loneliness can also cause new health concerns. It might be difficult to overcome the vicious cycle of loneliness brought on by chronic conditions, which can restrict social interaction.

Mitigating Loneliness for Better Well-Being:

1. **Cultivating Social Connections**: It is essential to actively seek out and cultivate social contacts. Joining clubs or groups, getting involved in social activities, and preserving relationships can all work as a protective barrier against the detrimental consequences of loneliness.

2. **Professional Support**: Getting professional assistance from therapists or counselors can be quite beneficial for people who are experiencing loneliness. In addition to offering resources for creating deep connections, therapeutic therapies can assist in addressing underlying emotional problems.

3. **Physical Activity**: Exercise on a regular basis has been demonstrated to improve mental and physical health. In addition to lowering stress, it also offers chances for social connection, which lessens feelings of isolation.

4. **Mindfulness and Self-Reflection**: A deeper comprehension of one's feelings and needs might result from engaging in activities like self-reflection and mindfulness. Addressing loneliness and creating a more fulfilled existence require this self-awareness.

Overall, loneliness has consequences that go well beyond its emotional impact. Our physical and mental well-being is deeply woven by loneliness, which has an impact on everything from cognitive performance to cardiovascular health. Understanding the deep effects of loneliness emphasizes how critical it is to take proactive measures to address it. People can escape the clutches of loneliness and start living a better, more connected life by making meaningful connections, getting help, and placing a high priority on their physical and mental well-being.

2: CAUSES OF LONELINESS

Numerous interrelated factors that permeate our lives and contribute to loneliness are the root causes of this ubiquitous and profoundly human feeling. Life transitions are one important aspect. Establishing social networks can be upended by significant life events like retiring, relocating to a different place, or ending a romantic relationship, leaving people feeling lost and alone in a strange and strange world. Being cut off from people and activities that one is accustomed to might lead to a deep sense of loneliness.

Another powerful factor is social isolation, which occurs when people don't have a strong social network or find it difficult to make meaningful relationships. Real face-to-face contacts are frequently replaced by the appearance of social engagement through computers in our hyper connected but paradoxically isolating digital age. Creating ways to prevent loneliness and promote a more connected and satisfying existence requires an understanding of these intricate and linked causes.

LIFE TRANSITIONS

Unavoidable and frequently difficult life transitions might serve as acute triggers for the onset of loneliness. These turning points in life, which might be brought about by a job change, moving to a new city, ending a relationship, or starting retirement, disrupt the comfortable routine of a person's life and create uncertainty and a feeling of isolation. During times of transition, the complex social network that formerly gave one a sense of belonging can suddenly come apart, leaving people struggling with a deep sense of isolation.

For example, moving to a new city might be an especially lonely experience. Getting around in a new place can be lonely because there aren't any familiar people or comfortable routines. The early stages of transition can heighten feelings of loneliness as people work to make new relationships, emphasizing the gap created by the loss of the familiar social network.

Similar to this, significant life events like retirement or the termination of a long-term relationship can force people into emotionally unfamiliar places. The transition from a communal life to a lonelier one can be disconcerting, frequently resulting in a feeling of isolation as people struggle with the absence of company and the reconstruction of their social personas.

It is imperative that folks who are undergoing life transitions and others who wish to offer support acknowledge the part that these changes play in perpetuating loneliness. An increasingly empathic approach is made possible by the realization that times of change may also be accompanied by increased feelings of isolation, highlighting the value of fostering social relationships during these turbulent times. People can negotiate life transitions with resilience by actively addressing the possibility of loneliness that comes with them. They can do this by looking for and making new connections that fit their changing circumstances.

SOCIAL ISOLATION

One of the main causes of loneliness is social isolation, which is caused by a lack of both quantity and quality of social contacts. It is frequently centered on a lack of meaningful interaction and true bonds rather than just physical seclusion. In the contemporary world, social isolation is paradoxically on the rise, despite the fact that digital connectivity can give the impression of companionship. Even in the midst of a sea of virtual pals, superficial online interactions may not offer the depth of connection necessary to ward off loneliness, leaving people feeling emotionally empty.

Furthermore, some life events—like retiring or losing a spouse—can make social isolation worse. One's social network may gradually deteriorate as a result of the decrease in regular social encounters that frequently coincide with these life transitions. People may find themselves navigating a more isolated existence without the regular social connections offered by work or shared interests, and this decrease in daily social interactions can greatly contribute to the beginning of loneliness. Understanding that social isolation is a major contributor to loneliness emphasizes the value of developing real connections and relationships that go beyond appearances in order to provide emotional support and a sense of belonging.

A single parent who has little assistance could feel lonely because they don't have a solid network of friends and family. Feeling alone and isolated while juggling parental duties without support or consistent adult engagement is a common occurrence. Emotional pressure might result from a lack of possibilities for socialization and experience sharing with other adults.

Socially anxious person: A person who suffers from social anxiety may isolate themselves by avoiding social interactions. People who struggle with social anxiety may find it difficult to interact with others, go to events, or establish lasting relationships due to their fear of being judged or evaluated negatively. Avoidance like this can lead to a vicious cycle of loneliness and increased anxiety.

People in Extended Quarantine: People who are placed in extended quarantine or isolation, perhaps in the event of a pandemic, may feel socially isolated. A lack of social interaction with friends, family, or the larger community can exacerbate feelings of loneliness and negatively affect mental health. Feelings of separation may be exacerbated by the lack of in-person connections.

Person Facing Discrimination: People who experience marginalization or discrimination due to their sexual orientation, gender, or race may withdraw themselves from society. Bias and prejudice can result in social exclusion, which makes it challenging for those affected to interact with others, build relationships, and take part in social activities.

New Immigrant Facing Language Barrier: A recent immigrant who is having trouble speaking the language may feel alone in society. Ineffective communication can make it more difficult for them to connect with others, form relationships, or take part in community events. A feeling of exclusion and loneliness may be exacerbated by a linguistic barrier.

TECHNOLOGY AND LONELINESS

In spite of its promise of never-before-seen connectedness, technology's ubiquitous presence paradoxically adds to the rising rate of loneliness in our contemporary society. In a world when social media, cellphones, and digital communication are omnipresent, the very devices meant to strengthen connections might unintentionally promote isolation. Online connections are maintained, with carefully selected photographs and status updates. This can lead to a false perception of others' lives and a heightened sense of inadequacy and feeling excluded.

Social media sites might foster loneliness even when

they offer opportunities for connection. A feeling of inadequacy and loneliness might result from constantly comparing oneself to others' supposedly active social life. Constant exposure to carefully constructed pictures of happy people and social interactions may worsen the emotional depths of loneliness because people internalize these pictures of themselves as being alone.

Furthermore, although they offer flexibility, the emergence of digital communication tools and remote work has the potential to blur the lines between personal and professional life. As the office, which was once a social hub, turns into a virtual setting where in-person interactions are being replaced by digital exchanges, the blurring of these lines may cause feelings of isolation. For people who thrive on the companionship of a physical workplace, the lack of water cooler talks and shared office experiences can be a major source of loneliness.

Identifying technology as a major contributor to loneliness is essential to creating solutions to lessen its effects. People can better negotiate the complexity of our interconnected yet fragmented world by maintaining a healthy relationship with technology and striking a balance between digital connectedness and intentional, face-to-face contact.

Technology can bring people together, but in some situations, it can also exacerbate feelings of loneliness. Here are some instances of how loneliness and technology may be related:

Social Media Comparisons: Social comparison and feelings of inadequacy might result from a constant exposure to well-chosen and idealized depictions of other people's lives on social media platforms. People may feel isolated and lonely because they believe that their own lives are not as meaningful as others.

Cyber bullying and Cyber Harassment: Negative social interactions, like cyber bullying and cyber harassment, can take place online thanks to technology. These kinds of activities can cause people to retreat from online communities, which can result in feelings of loneliness and isolation. Technology's ability to give anonymity can occasionally make these problems worse.

Digital Shallow Connections: Although technology makes communication quick and simple, it also has the potential to foster relationships that are more surface-level. Even while people have a lot of online contacts, constant digital communication may not have the intimacy and depth of face-to-face conversations, leaving them feeling lonely.

Virtual Overload and Diminished Face-to-Face Interaction: An excessive dependence on digital communication could result in a decrease in in-person encounters. Excessive time spent in virtual environments can deteriorate interpersonal connections and heighten feelings of isolation and detachment from reality.

Digital Diversion in Real Environments: In real-world social contexts, technology can occasionally be a distraction. For instance, those who are always staring at their phones during social events may pass up chances to make real connections. Even in social situations, this diversion might make one feel alone.

It's important to remember that although technology can exacerbate loneliness, when utilized purposefully and wisely, it can also be an incredibly effective tool for building relationships. Achieving equilibrium and being cognizant of the possible detrimental effects of technology on social welfare can assist people in developing more meaningful and healthy connections.

MENTAL HEALTH AND LONELINESS

An individual's well-being can be greatly impacted by the complicated interplay that exists between loneliness and mental health. Frequently written off as a transient emotional state, loneliness can develop into a chronic illness with serious consequences for mental health. The lack of significant relationships and social support can serve as a trigger for a number of mental health conditions, such as anxiety, sadness, and elevated stress levels.

The emotional toll might be especially high for people who are experiencing chronic loneliness. Depressing sensations can arise or worsen as a result of persistent feelings of loneliness, which can also cause pessimism and despair. The loneliness that frequently follows isolation may heighten anxiety as people struggle with social anxiety and rejection worries, making it more difficult for them to make new friends.

Furthermore, loneliness may have a major role in the emergence or aggravation of diseases linked to stress. Chronic stress brought on by loneliness can have physiological effects, raising cortisol levels and perhaps interfering with sleep cycles. This kind of stress can weaken the immune system over time, increasing a person's vulnerability to many health problems and negatively impacting their mental health.

Pre-existing mental health issues, on the other hand, can contribute to an increased experience of loneliness. People who suffer from mental health disorders like depression or social anxiety may find it difficult to make and keep friends, which can create a vicious cycle where loneliness and mental health issues feed off one another.

Solving the mental health nexus requires a multifaceted strategy. Developing social networks, getting help from professionals, and putting self-care first is essential for reducing the negative impact of loneliness on mental health. Counseling and support groups are two examples of therapeutic interventions that can give people useful tools to help them manage the emotional difficulties of loneliness, build resilience, and advance mental health.

Individuals, communities, and healthcare providers must all understand and acknowledge the complex relationship between mental health and loneliness. We may try to create a more compassionate and supportive environment that uplifts individuals' mental health and develops genuine connections by developing empathy, lowering stigma surrounding mental health difficulties, and proactively addressing the fundamental causes of loneliness.

There is a close relationship between loneliness and mental health, with loneliness frequently causing or aggravating mental health issues. Here are some instances of how mental health may be impacted by loneliness:

Depression: One of the main risk factors for depression is ongoing loneliness. Depressive symptoms can arise or intensify as a result of feelings of loneliness, a lack of social support system, and a perception of having few meaningful relationships. Experiencing loneliness can exacerbate depressing and gloomy feelings.

Anxiety Disorders: The onset or aggravation of anxiety disorders might be attributed to loneliness. People may become more anxious in social settings due to a fear of social rejection or judgment, which isolates them even more. Prolonged isolation can exacerbate panic attacks, social anxiety, or generalized anxiety.

Low Self-Esteem: Prolonged isolation can damage one's sense of value and self-esteem. People who experience social isolation could internalize self-defeating thoughts, which lowers their sense of worth and confidence. A vicious cycle of loneliness and mental health issues can be exacerbated by low self-esteem.

Elevated Stress Levels: There is a correlation between loneliness and elevated stress levels. People may find it harder to manage challenges in life if they lack emotional support and social support. In consequence, long-term stress can exacerbate a number of mental health conditions, such as mood disorders and burnout.

Suicidal Thoughts and Behaviors: Suicidal thoughts and behaviors may be brought on by extreme and protracted loneliness. Some people may consider self-harming activities or act on their feelings of hopelessness and despair when they feel alone. In these situations, supportive relationships and interventions are essential.

3: CONSEQUENCES OF CHRONIC LONELINESS

Chronic loneliness has far-reaching implications that go beyond simply emotional discomfort, infiltrating numerous parts of a person's life and general well-being. The long-term effects of prolonged isolation can be significant and varied, affecting everything from mental health to physical health.

MENTAL HEALTH IMPLICATIONS:

- **Depression and Anxiety**: Chronic loneliness is a significant risk factor for depression and anxiety disorders. A prolonged sensation of isolation and separation might contribute to a negative spiral of thoughts and emotions.
- Cognitive Decline: According to research, there may be a link between chronic loneliness and cognitive decline, including an increased risk of illnesses such as Alzheimer's disease and other types of dementia.
- Heightened Stress Levels: Loneliness-related stress can trigger an excessive stress response, contributing to higher cortisol levels. Chronic stress can harm both mental and physical health.

PHYSICAL HEALTH CONSEQUENCES:

- Cardiovascular Issues: Individuals who are chronically lonely may be at a higher risk of cardiovascular disease. Loneliness can cause increased stress, which can lead to high blood pressure and other cardiovascular problems.
- Weakened Immune System: Loneliness is associated with a reduced immune system, making people more prone to infections and illnesses.
- Sleep Disturbances: Sleep difficulties are frequently associated with chronic loneliness. Prolonged isolation might result in insomnia, trouble falling asleep, or disturbing sleep patterns.

BEHAVIORAL CONSEQUENCES:

People who are lonely may exhibit a range of behavioral effects that affect how they relate to others and to themselves. Following are a few typical behavioral outcomes linked to loneliness:

- Substance Abuse: Some people may turn to substances such as alcohol or drugs to cope with the emotional pain of loneliness, increasing the risk of substance abuse and addiction.
- Social Withdrawal: People who are lonely frequently experience social withdrawal, in which case they may purposefully avoid social situations. One factor that might lead to self-imposed isolation and restrict participation in social activities and events is fear of rejection or a feeling of not belonging.
- Decreased Communication: People who are lonely may communicate less with others in person and online. Reduced efforts to start or continue discussions might result from a perceived lack of social support, which feeds the cycle of isolation.

- Negative Emotional Expressions: People's emotional expressions can be impacted by loneliness. Some people may display more negative emotions as a mirror of their internal emotional condition, such as irritation, annoyance, or melancholy. The way that people interact with one another can be affected by these expressions.

- Avoidance of Eye Contact: Avoiding eye contact is a typical social cue and has been linked to loneliness. Those who experience loneliness could avoid eye contact to save themselves from possible rejection or social discomfort.

- Impaired Social Skills: Prolonged isolation can have an adverse effect on the growth of social skills. People may find it difficult to read social cues, start and sustain conversations, and comprehend the subtleties of interpersonal relationships.

- Growing Dependency on Technology: Loneliness may cause a person to rely too much on digital communication at the expense of in-person relationships, even if technology can foster a sense of connectedness. The depth and caliber of relationships may suffer as a result of this behavioral change

- Unhealthy Coping Mechanisms: Chronic loneliness can lead to the development of unhealthy coping methods, such as overeating or under-eating, which can have a negative impact on overall physical health.

- Risk-Taking activities: Risk-taking activities can be a coping mechanism or a means of escaping loneliness for certain people. This can involve abusing drugs or alcohol, acting carelessly, or making snap decisions that seem good at the time but may turn out to be harmful.

- Emotional Eating or Appetite Loss: Emotional eating can be influenced by loneliness. While some people may lose their appetite as a result of the emotional anguish connected to isolation, others may turn to emotional eating as a coping mechanism for feelings of loneliness.

- Challenges in Building Relationships: Being alone can make it difficult to start new relationships. People could find it difficult to connect with people, make new friends, or take part in activities that promote relationship development.

IMPACT ON RELATIONSHIPS:

- Negative Social Interactions: Chronic loneliness's emotional strain can occasionally appear in bad social interactions. Individuals may struggle with social skills, which can lead to increased isolation as interpersonal ties deteriorate.

Negative social interactions can have detrimental effects on individuals' well-being and contribute to feelings of distress or discomfort. Here are two examples of negative social interactions:

Bullying: Bullying is defined as a pattern of hurtful behavior meant to inflict pain, discomfort, or an imbalance of power. It can happen in a variety of settings, such as internet forums, workplaces, or educational institutions. Bullying can take many different forms, such as physical intimidation, social isolation, verbal abuse, and rumors. Bullying causes feelings of dread, loneliness, and low self-esteem in the targeted person, which has a detrimental effect on their mental and emotional health.

Small-scale assaults: These are subtly offensive, frequently inadvertent comments or actions that denigrate or marginalize people because of their gender, race, ethnicity, or other traits. These acts may consist of offensive remarks, prejudices, or actions that exclude others. Even while those who perpetrate tiny insults might not be aware of their effects, the cumulative effect on the recipient may increase worry, stress, and a feeling of alienation.

- Cycles of Isolation: Loneliness can set in motion a self-perpetuating cycle in which the individual's isolation becomes a barrier to making new connections. Loneliness might make it difficult to engage in fulfilling relationships.

IMPACT ON OVERALL WELL-BEING:

Lower Life Satisfaction: Chronic loneliness is frequently linked to lower life satisfaction and overall well-being. A lack of meaningful connections can lead to feelings of unfulfillment and discontent with life.

Understanding and resolving the repercussions of chronic loneliness necessitate a multifaceted strategy that takes into account both mental and physical well-being. Interventions that promote social connection, mental health support, and lifestyle changes can help to mitigate the negative consequences of extended isolation, resulting in a healthier and more connected existence.

4: OVERCOMING LONELINESS
Techniques and Strategies

As a common human experience, loneliness can be a profound and difficult emotion to deal with. Overcoming loneliness requires a multimodal approach that incorporates techniques that deal with the psychological, social, and emotional aspects of this complex phenomenon. In this exploration, we explore four essential strategies for overcoming loneliness: increasing self-awareness, forming healthy habits, pursuing interests and hobbies, and getting professional assistance.

BUILDING SELF-AWARENESS:
(Unraveling the Layers of Loneliness)

Understanding the root causes of loneliness allows individuals to confront and challenge negative self-perceptions, paving the way for a more positive self-concept. Building self-awareness is a foundational step in overcoming loneliness. It involves a deep and honest exploration of one's emotions, thought patterns, and underlying beliefs that may contribute to feelings of isolation.

Recognizing the impact of past experiences on current emotional states is also part of self-awareness. Unresolved traumas, attachment patterns, or past rejections can all influence how people perceive themselves and relate to others. By acknowledging and addressing these underlying issues, people can gradually release the emotional burdens that contribute to loneliness.

Mindfulness, through practices like meditation, fosters an awareness of the present moment, allowing people to detach from distressing thoughts and emotions associated with loneliness. Developing self-awareness is an essential component of human growth.

The following are some instances of techniques and activities that people can engage in to improve their self-awareness:

Journaling: Keeping a journal enables people to consider their feelings, ideas, and experiences. Writing about everyday experiences, obstacles, and successes on a regular basis might help one become more self-aware by revealing behavioral patterns and reoccurring themes.

Meditation with awareness: In mindfulness meditation, you focus on the current moment while letting go of any judgment. Techniques like body scans and concentrated breathing can increase awareness of one's thoughts and feelings and foster a deeper comprehension of one's inner experiences.

Personality tests: Taking tests like the Big Five Personality Traits or the Myers-Briggs Type Indicator (MBTI) can reveal a person's preferences, strong points, and possible growth areas. Being conscious of one's personality can help one become more self-aware.

360-Degree Feedback: Getting input from friends, family, coworkers, and peers offers a more comprehensive view of one's areas of strength and growth. A 360-degree feedback approach can assist people in seeing themselves from other people's perspectives.

Exercises for Emotional Intelligence: Focusing on developing emotional intelligence through activities like labeling and identifying emotions can help people become more self-aware. The secret to personal development is comprehending how emotions affect conduct and judgment.

Therapy or Counseling: Under the supervision of a qualified expert, professional therapy or counseling offers a secure environment in which one can examine their thoughts, feelings, and behaviors. Therapy might greatly benefit in finding underlying patterns and increasing self-awareness.

Reflective Practices: Whether done daily or once a week, setting aside time for deliberate thought enables people to evaluate their deeds, choices, and responses. One way to engage in reflective activities is to pose challenging questions to oneself regarding goals and reasons.

Feedback Loops in Goal planning: Including feedback loops in goal planning might be beneficial. A deeper grasp of one's own goals and the variables impacting achievement can be attained by routinely reviewing progress, making goal adjustments, and thinking back on failures.

Active Listening: Engaging in conversations with others while actively listening can help people become more conscious of their communication style and how they interact with diverse viewpoints. Being attentive of both spoken and nonverbal clues helps one become more self-aware.

Regular Check-Ins: Setting aside time for regular self-check-ins allows individuals to assess their overall well-being, satisfaction with life, and alignment with personal values. These check-ins can provide valuable insights into areas that may require attention or adjustment.

DEVELOPING HEALTHY HABITS:
(Nurturing the Body and Mind)

Loneliness is inevitably linked to physical and mental well-being, and developing healthy habits contributes not only to a sense of vitality but also to improved mood and adaptability. Regular exercise, balanced nutrition, and adequate sleep all play important roles in fostering overall well-being and combating the negative effects of loneliness.

Physical activity, in particular, has been shown to have profound effects on mental health, releasing endorphins, the body's natural mood elevators, and providing an opportunity for social interaction if done in group settings. Incorporating exercise into daily routines can serve as a powerful antidote to the lethargy and isolation often associated with loneliness.

A well-balanced diet also improves brain function and helps regulate mood. Ensuring that the body receives vital nutrients contributes to emotional resilience, minimizing susceptibility to emotions of loneliness and despair.

Sleep deprivation may aggravate feelings of loneliness and contribute to increased stress levels. Establishing consistent sleep patterns and creating a sleep-conducive environment are essential components of nurturing both physical and mental well-being.

ENGAGING IN HOBBIES AND INTERESTS:
(Cultivating Passion and Connection)

Hobbies and interests provide avenues for self-expression, skill development, and social connection, and provide a sense of purpose and fulfillment, counteracting the void that loneliness often brings. Whether it is artistic pursuits, sports, or intellectual endeavors, cultivating passions contributes to a more enriching and connected life.

Participating in group activities centered on shared interests allows for social interaction in a context where individuals can bond over a common passion. Joining clubs, classes, or online communities related to personal interests opens doors to meeting like-minded individuals, fostering connections that go beyond the surface level.

Hobbies provide a sense of accomplishment and self-worth, nurturing a positive self-image that counteracts the negative impact of loneliness. They allow individuals to allocate time for activities that bring joy and fulfillment, shifting the focus away from loneliness and towards personal growth.

SEEKING PROFESSIONAL HELP:
(Navigating Loneliness with Support)

Seeking help from mental health specialists provides an organized and supportive setting for addressing loneliness and its underlying causes, especially when it is entrenched or linked to deeper emotional concerns.

Individual and group therapy both provide a confidential space for people to explore and process their emotions. Therapists can help people build coping mechanisms, reframing negative thought patterns, and developing strategies for improving interpersonal skills. Group therapy, in particular, provides the added benefit of connecting with others who may have had similar experiences, fostering a sense of community and understanding.

Loneliness and mental health conditions such as depression or anxiety can coexist in some cases, and a mental health professional can conduct assessments, provide diagnoses, and tailor interventions to address both the loneliness and the underlying mental health issues. Medication may be considered in some cases, and psychiatrists can collaborate with individuals to determine appropriate treatment plans.

Furthermore, support groups that are specifically focused on loneliness or related mental health challenges can be valuable resources, as they allow individuals to share their experiences, receive support, and gain insights into overcoming loneliness from others who may be on similar journeys.

INTEGRATION OF STRATEGIES:
(Crafting a Holistic Approach)

Building self-awareness, developing healthy habits, engaging in hobbies, and seeking professional help are not isolated actions but components of a holistic approach to well-being that must be integrated to be effective in overcoming loneliness.

Self-awareness, for example, can inform the selection of hobbies that align with personal values and interests, resulting in a more authentic and fulfilling engagement; similarly, healthy habits such as regular exercise can serve as both a means of combating loneliness and a conduit for social connection when pursued in group settings.

By combining these strategies, people can address loneliness holistically, recognizing the connections between the social, emotional, and physical aspects of their lives. A holistic approach acknowledges that the process of overcoming loneliness is dynamic and ongoing, requiring self-compassion, adaptability, and a commitment to personal growth.

A JOURNEY TOWARDS CONNECTION AND FULFILLMENT

Through self-awareness, healthy habits, hobbies, and professional help when necessary, people can navigate the complexities of loneliness and create a path towards sustained well-being. Overcoming loneliness is a deeply personal and transformative process that requires self-discovery, intentional choices, and a commitment to building a life rich in connection and meaning.

Although loneliness is a universal experience, there are as many different strategies for overcoming loneliness as there are people who experience it. By combining these strategies, people can create a life that goes beyond the confines of isolation and embraces a tapestry of relationships, self-discovery, and personal fulfillment. Overcoming loneliness is more than just looking for a way to connect; it is a deep investigation of one's own fortitude, resilience, and potential for growth.

5: MAKING LIKE MINDED FRIENDS

Making friends with similar interests may be a rewarding and meaningful experience. Connecting with others who have similar interests, values, and passions can result in meaningful relationships and a sense of belonging. Here are some ideas for making like-minded friends:

Identify Your Interests:

Consider your interests, emotions, and values. What activities make you happy and fulfilled? Understanding your interests is the first step in meeting people who share your interests.

Attend Events and Activities:

Participate in clubs, classes, or events that are linked to your interests. Attend courses, seminars, or gatherings where individuals who share your interests assemble. This allows you to meet possible friends in an environment where you already have a common interest.

Meeting others who are passionate about the same things you are, whether professionally or personally, can happen at conferences and expos relating to your field of interest. Make the most of the chance to network at these events.

Online Communities:

Search online platforms and communities that are related to your hobbies. Join social media groups, forums, or communities where people talk about and share information about topics that interest you. This can be a terrific method to connect with like-minded people all across the world.

Volunteer for Causes:

Participate in voluntary activities that align with your ideals. Volunteering, whether for environmental protection, social justice, or animal welfare, can link you with people who share your desire to make a difference.

Take Classes or Workshops:

Enroll in classes or workshops based on your interests. This can range from art classes to coding sessions. Learning alongside individuals who share similar interests creates a natural setting for making connections.

Be Open and Approachable:

We must approach social interactions with a positive attitude and an open Smile, strike up a conversation, and show genuine interest in others. Being approachable makes it easy for others who share your interests to connect with you.

Attend Meetups or Networking Events:

Attend local meetups or networking events that are relevant to your interests. These gatherings are intended to let individuals meet, share ideas, and form relationships. It's a great way to meet others who share your passions.

Be Patient and Persistent:

Friendships take time to develop, so be patient. Attend events on a regular basis, participate in debates, and take the time to get to know people. Friendships are typically formed gradually, so don't be disheartened if relationships do not form right away.

Utilize Social Media:

Use social media channels to connect with people who share your interests. Follow relevant hash tags, join relevant groups, and participate in discussions. Online interactions can lead to offline friendships.

Host Gatherings:

Make an effort to organize gatherings or activities focusing on your interests. This not only allows you to communicate your passion, but it also attracts people who are likely to share your interests.

Keep in mind that friendship is a two-way street. When looking for like-minded friends, be open to different points of view and be a supportive friend in return. When people share true interests and principles, they frequently form genuine-ties.

6: NAVIGATING GENUINE RELATIONSHIPS

Explore the complexities of developing and maintaining authentic relationships in a world filled with both physical and digital interactions as we embark on a journey towards meaningful connections. This guide will help you understand the fundamentals of true connections and build a sense of belonging in your personal and digital spheres.

Navigating true relationships is an art that requires authenticity, sensitivity, and a dedication to mutual progress. A genuine connection is built on open communication and vulnerability, allowing individuals to disclose their true selves without fear of criticism. Active listening is essential for creating an environment in which everyone feels heard and understood.

Meaningful relationships are built on trust, which is gradually gained via reliability, honesty, and consistency. It requires openness as well as the readiness to be emotionally present. Reciprocity, which guarantees that efforts, consideration, and support are returned in kind, is another crucial component.

In the digital age, it is crucial to strike a healthy balance between in-person and virtual friendships. While virtual communication facilitates relationships, in-person friendships require time to create intimacy and deeper understanding.Respect for each others personalities, personal space, and ideals build a strong foundation for long term engagement.

Genuine relationships, in the end, are built on mutual respect, understanding, and shared values, and navigating these connections requires continual self-reflection, adaptability, and a commitment to establishing an atmosphere in which both people may thrive genuinely and happily.

Building Trust: Discover the foundations of trust and how it forms the bedrock of any genuine relationship, as well as practical strategies for establishing trust with others and deepening your connections. Trust is the bedrock upon which deep connections are formed, fostering a sense of security and mutual understanding.

Trust is the base upon which strong connections is created, establishing a sense of security and mutual understanding. Building trust is the cornerstone of true relationships, a delicate process that unfolds through shared experiences, authenticity, and emotional vulnerability.

Open Communication: Individuals in real relationships openly communicate their thoughts, feelings, and worries, creating an environment where both sides feel heard and respected. Honest talks provide the framework for trust to thrive.

Consistency and Reliability: Following through on commitments and being dependable in both small and significant matters demonstrates a genuine investment in the relationship. Reliability creates a sense of security, reinforcing the belief that one can rely on the other person.

Emotional Availability: Genuine relationships thrive when individuals feel comfortable expressing vulnerability without fear of judgment, and sharing both joys and sorrows establishes an emotional connection that grows stronger over time.

Setting and Respecting Boundaries: Understanding and accepting each other's limits develops a sense of respect and safety within the partnership, and clear communication about personal boundaries aids in the creation of an atmosphere of trust and mutual understanding.

Forgiveness and Repair: Mistakes will inevitably occur in any relationship; trust-building entails the ability for forgiveness and the resolve to mend ruptures. Acknowledging mistakes, accepting responsibility, and actively working toward resolution all contribute to the resilience of trust.

Shared Experiences: Building a reservoir of memories and reinforcing the sense of connection through shared hobbies, adventures, or facing challenges together, these shared moments contribute to the depth of the relationship and solidify the bonds of trust. Building trust is a continuous, evolving process that requires time, commitment, and a genuine investment in the well-being of the relationship.

Effective Communication

Explore active listening, nonverbal cues, and the power of empathy to improve the quality of your interactions. Effective communication is the lifeblood of genuine relationships, providing the arteries through which understanding, empathy, and connection flow. It entails more than just the exchange of words; it includes active listening, empathy, and the ability to convey thoughts and emotions authentically.

Active listening, in which individuals not only hear words but also comprehend the underlying emotions, fosters a deeper connection and requires presence, a willingness to engage, and an openness to truly understand the other person's perspective.

Genuine communication entails being open about both joys and challenges, creating a space where individuals can express their authentic selves without fear of judgment. Sharing thoughts, feelings, and concerns with honesty and vulnerability establishes trust and strengthens the emotional bonds within the relationship.

Furthermore, effective communication in true relationships necessitates clarity and intention; clearly articulating concepts, asking clarifying questions, and providing constructive feedback all contribute to an environment in which both people feel heard and appreciated.

Finally, successful communication bridges the gap between individuals, developing a connection that goes beyond words and creating a common understanding that provides the foundation of long-lasting, meaningful friendships.

Balancing Independence and Connection

Explore the delicate dance of keeping one's identity while building meaningful connections, as well as the significance of personal boundaries and how they contribute to flourishing relationships.

Genuine authenticity thrives when people are secure in their independence yet willingly weave their lives with a partner. Balancing independence and connection in genuine relationships is a delicate dance, requiring a nuanced understanding of individual needs and a mutual commitment to personal growth within the context of a shared journey.

Keeping oneself intact in a relationship is vital for personal fulfillment. Sincere relationships flourish when both partners follow their passions, develop their own interests, and keep evolving personally. This independence benefits each partner individually and adds to the dynamic of the relationship.

Fostering connection entails sharing experiences, supporting one another, and working together to create a shared narrative that unites two distinct life stories. At the same time, it necessitates being emotionally present and aware of the needs of the other person.

The key to striking a balance between autonomy and connection is effective communication. Expressing one's needs, boundaries, and goals makes the other person feel seen and understood. Respecting one another's independence while actively engaging in shared experiences fosters a harmonious balance where autonomy and connection coexist, fostering a sincere relationship that enables each person to thrive separately and together.

Recognizing and Addressing Toxic Relationships

Prioritize your well-being and cultivate healthier connections by arming yourself with the knowledge and skills necessary to recognize toxic aspects in relationships and discover practical solutions to deal with and overcome these obstacles.

In order to cultivate real connections, it is critical to identify and deal with toxic relationships. To safeguard both the relationship's health and the individual's wellbeing, it is critical to recognize toxic relationships and take proactive measures to protect them.

Recognizing Toxicity: Toxic elements in a relationship can be recognized by being aware of exhibiting negative patterns. These patterns can include constant lack of support, manipulation, verbal or emotional abuse, control problems, or a generalized feeling of dread and unease. It is important to follow your gut and pay attention to how the relationship makes you feel both mentally and emotionally.

Establishing Boundaries: One of the most important things to do when dealing with toxicity is to communicate personal limits, expectations, and values. Boundaries serve as a protective barrier against abuse or manipulation and provide a framework for relationships that are courteous and well-balanced.

Communication: Toxin removal necessitates direct and honest communication. It is important to communicate worries, emotions, and boundaries in order to build mutual understanding. However, good communication also entails active listening and being receptive to the other person's point of view. These discussions must be conducted with empathy and a shared goal of repairing the relationship.

Seeking Support: Seeking support from friends, family, or professionals can offer an outside perspective and emotional guidance. Support systems can offer validation, encouragement, and useful advice on navigating the complexities of toxic relationships. In some cases, toxicity may persist despite efforts to address it within the relationship.

Choosing Self-Care: In the end, identifying and dealing with toxic relationships frequently require making tough choices. Putting one's health first may entail establishing clear boundaries, getting professional assistance, or, in the worst situations, ending the relationship. Choosing self-care is an expression of self-love and opens the door to personal development and the development of healthier relationships.

The pursuit of authentic relationships requires the guts to identify and deal with toxicity. It is an active commitment to creating spaces in which people can grow mentally, emotionally, and spiritually, building bonds based on mutual respect, understanding, and personal development.

Digital Connections: Finding Meaningful Relationships

Explore the distinct dynamics of virtual relationships in a globalized world. Learn how to build authentic connections on the internet while weighing the advantages and possible drawbacks of the virtual environment.

Digital connections have become an essential part of how we establish and maintain relationships in our increasingly connected world. Although the digital sphere presents previously unheard-of opportunities for connectivity, the difficulty is navigating these virtual spaces to foster relationships that are not only practical but profoundly meaningful.

The Landscape of Digital Connections: Social media interactions, online communities, virtual friendships, and even romantic relationships started through dating apps are examples of the wide range of digital connections that exist. One of the main draws of these digital spaces is their accessibility, which allows people to connect with people who are geographically distant from them and who have similar interests or experiences.

Building Genuine Connections Online: Intentionality and authenticity are key factors in the development of genuine relationships, despite the frequently expressed worries about the shallowness of digital connections. People who are looking to make meaningful connections online should approach these interactions with the same openness and sincerity that they would in person.

Common Interests and Communities: Digital platforms present a multitude of venues for people to come together around common interests, pastimes, or passions. Participating in online communities or forums devoted to particular subjects gives like-minded people a way to meet, exchange stories, and form bonds based on common ground.

Social Media and Authenticity: Even though social media has come under fire for encouraging carefully controlled and filtered versions of reality, it can also serve as a platform for real connections: sharing real parts of one's life, having deep conversations, and actively participating in other people's digital lives can all result in the development of meaningful online friendships.

Navigating Dating Apps: Digital connections have brought about a significant transformation in the field of romantic relationships, thanks in large part to dating apps. Although these platforms are sometimes linked to casual encounters, many people have found meaningful and long-lasting connections through digital dating; the secret is to be transparent about one's intentions, communicate honestly, and invest the time to get to know potential partners beyond their digital persona.

Challenges of Digital Connections: Although there is room for real relationships in the digital sphere, there are obstacles to overcome. For example, the lack of physical presence can impede the depth of emotional connection. People frequently make mistakes, run the risk of lying, and have a tendency to value quantity over quality when interacting with others online.

Nurturing Digital Relationships: A combination of virtual and real-world interaction is needed to foster digital relationships. Although the initial contact can take place online, face-to-face interactions—such as video conferences or in-person meetings—must be made in order to further develop the relationship. By taking this hybrid approach, it is possible to guarantee that digital connections develop into relationships based on both the virtual and tangible facets of life.

The Role of Trust and Transparency: In the digital sphere, where people may present edited versions of themselves, trust must be built through transparency. In digital interactions, authenticity—that is, being truthful about one's identity, intentions, and feelings—creates a sense of trust that serves as the foundation for meaningful relationships.

Balancing Quantity and Quality: The digital world tends to place more emphasis on the quantity than the quality of connections. People who are looking for real relationships have to fight the temptation to accumulate a lot of online contacts at the expense of meaningful interaction. Having a few deep connections is usually more fulfilling than having a lot of shallow ones.

Digital Etiquette and Respect: While thoughtful and considerate online behavior contributes to the creation of a positive and supportive digital environment, respecting others' boundaries, engaging in active listening, and understanding the subtleties of digital communication are all essential to developing and sustaining genuine relationships online.

The Evolution of Digital Connections: Virtual reality, augmented reality, and other emerging technologies promise more immersive and enriching online experiences, and as technology advances, so too will the landscape of digital connections. That being said, no matter what tools we have at our disposal, the fundamental values of intentionality, authenticity, and respect will remain crucial for fostering authentic relationships in the digital age.

To sum up, meaningful relationships can definitely flourish in the digital sphere. Whether people are connecting through common interests, making friends on social media, or figuring out the ins and outs of digital dating, people can create connections that go beyond the virtual. The secret is to approach digital relationships with the same sincerity and intentionality that define relationships in person. This will open up the possibility of real and satisfying connections in the constantly growing digital sphere.

7: DIGITAL CONNECTIONS

(Finding meaningful relationships online)

This exploration delves into the intricacies of digital connections, focusing on safe online platforms, strategies for genuine connections, and the importance of maintaining healthy boundaries in the digital landscape. In the rapidly changing digital age, online platforms have redefined how we connect, communicate, and form relationships. The internet, once a realm primarily for information exchange, has become a vast social landscape where individuals can forge connections, share experiences, and build meaningful relationships. However, the digital realm also poses challenges, from issues of safety to the potential for superficial interactions.

SAFE ONLINE PLATFORMS:

Navigating the Digital Terrain

Many platforms are available in the digital world to help people connect, ranging from social media behemoths to specialized communities built around common interests. But not all online environments are made equal, and maintaining safety is crucial when trying to build meaningful relationships. In this article, we will look at what makes a safe online platform and offer some examples of how it works.

Characteristics of Safe Online Platforms:

1. **Privacy Protections:** Safe online platforms put the privacy of their users first. They utilize strong security features, such encryption, to protect user data and guarantee that private information is kept private.

2. **Moderation and Policies:** A secure environment is created by platforms that have clear community norms and effective moderation. These methods help prevent hate speech, harassment, and other harmful conduct, making the user base feel comfortable.

3. **User Verification:** Certain platforms have user verification procedures in place to verify users' identities. This reduces the possibility of users coming into contact with unknown or malevolent parties and fosters a sense of trust between users.

4. **Transparent Reporting Mechanisms:** Safe platforms enable users to take charge of their online experience and foster a responsive and accountable online community by giving them simple reporting options for offensive or harmful information.

5. **Education and Resources:** Safety-focused platforms frequently offer their users instructional materials. These materials might contain rules about proper online conduct, advice on identifying and avoiding frauds, and details on best practices for digital security.

Examples of Safe Online Platforms:

1. **LinkedIn:** Professional networking site LinkedIn places a strong emphasis on connection-building and user authenticity in a professional setting. It uses privacy settings, promotes the use of real names, and provides features like endorsements to bolster trustworthiness.

2. **Bumble:** One dating app that stands out is called Bumble. It encourages women to initiate contact and

includes safety measures like photo verification to build user confidence and guarantee authentic profiles.

3. **Quora:** Quora is a question-and-answer website that is best suited for meaningful interactions and information exchange. Its robust moderation system allows users to participate in thoughtful conversations in a polite and supportive community.

4. **Calm Community:** The community component of the meditation and mental health app Calm, which is based on mindfulness, highlights interactions that are constructive and encouraging. The platform promotes sincere relationships that are oriented toward well-being.

5. **Meetup:** Meetup allows offline, in-person encounters between people who share like interests, and the platform encourages community building by including safety elements such as user reviews and event host screening.

Strategies for Building Genuine Connections: Beyond the Digital Surface

Intentional strategies that go beyond surface-level interactions are necessary to build genuine connections online. These strategies range from fostering authenticity to using technology mindfully. The digital realm, with its abundance of information and stimuli, can occasionally foster shallow interactions.

Authenticity, empathy, and a desire to put in time and effort into relationships are necessary for creating meaningful connections. Here are two tactics to help you create sincere connections:

A] Active Listening: A key tactic for creating sincere connections is active listening. It entails paying close attention to what the other person is saying and comprehending it, all the while refraining from mentally preparing a reply. Put the following actions into practice:

Give Your Whole Attention: To demonstrate that you are completely present during a conversation, put away electronic devices and make eye contact.

B] Vulnerability and Authenticity: Being honest and forthright about your personal experiences, emotions, and ideas is frequently necessary to forging true connections. When you show vulnerability, you foster an atmosphere where people are at ease to be authentic. Think about the following:

Tell Personal Tales: When it's suitable, relate personal tales or experiences to the subject of discussion. This makes you seem like a genuine, approachable person to others.

Express Sincere Feelings: Don't be scared to be honest in how you communicate your feelings. Experiencing joy, enthusiasm, or vulnerability—letting people see your true feelings encourages a closer bond.

Admit Your Errors and Flaws: Since nobody is flawless, admitting your personal flaws can help you come off as more relatable. It demonstrates humility and an eagerness to develop.

Fostering Authenticity:

>**Authentic Self-Presentation:** Genuine connections are built on authenticity. People who are looking for meaningful interactions online are urged to be themselves, displaying their personalities, interests, and values in an unadorned manner.

>*Example:* On a forum for sharing photographs, a user openly reveals not just their greatest shots but also the difficulties and lessons they have learned along the way.

>**Open and Honest Communication:** Transparent communication is essential for meaningful connections. Sincere expression of thoughts and feelings during open and honest talks adds to the richness of digital relationships.

Example: Members of an online support group communicate honestly about their challenges and successes, fostering an environment where empathy and understanding are fostered by sincerity.

MINDFUL TECHNOLOGY USE:

Balancing Online and Offline Interactions: A more comprehensive social experience is achieved by using technology as a tool to augment, not replace, in-person relationships, even though digital connections are valuable. It is also important to strike a balance between online and offline encounters.

Example: Through an online hobby group, a user makes connections with like-minded people and then plans in-person get-togethers to deepen those relationships.

Setting Technology Boundaries: A healthier and more sustainable digital lifestyle is promoted by setting clear boundaries surrounding technology use, allocating specified times for online activities, and taking deliberate pauses. These measures help minimize digital tiredness and burnout.

Example: In order to make time for other activities and avoid the possible detrimental effects of excessive screen time, a user establishes a daily limit for social media use.

ACTIVELY PARTICIPATING IN COMMUNITIES:

1. **Engagement over Passive Consumption:** Engaging in online communities actively, as opposed to passively consuming content strengthens digital bonds. Participating in conversations, exchanging stories, and offering assistance to people in a community all enhance one's feeling of community.

   Example: Beyond just having a mutual interest in

books, members of a book club build a sense of community through actively participating in conversations, offering personal views, and working together to plan virtual activities.

2. **Seeking Quality Over Quantity:** A more meaningful online experience can be achieved by placing an emphasis on the quality of connections rather than the amount of followers or friends. Developing a smaller, more active network enables more genuine connections and deeper conversations.

   Example: Instead of prioritizing raw volume of views, a content producer prioritizes developing sincere relationships with a more intimate following.

MAINTAINING HEALTHY BOUNDARIES:

Navigating the Digital Landscape Safely

Setting and enforcing boundaries is essential for protecting personal well-being and guaranteeing positive online experiences. This section discusses the significance of boundary-setting and offers strategies for safely navigating the digital landscape. Although the digital landscape offers many opportunities for connection, it also poses challenges in maintaining healthy boundaries.

Importance of Healthy Boundaries:

1. **Protecting Mental and Emotional Well-Being:** Maintaining a positive online presence requires protecting mental and emotional well-being, which is shielded from the negative impacts of online interactions such as cyber bullying, excessive comparison, and information overload through healthy boundaries.

   Example: When embarking on a fitness journey, a user places restrictions around exposure to specific kinds of information that could cause them to feel bad about themselves; instead, they concentrate on finding sources of inspiration and support.

2. **Preserving Personal Privacy:** In the digital age, where information sharing is commonplace, boundaries protect individual privacy. A sense of security is enhanced by selectively sharing information online and by safeguarding important details.

Example: To manage the availability of personal information and restrict access to a trusted audience, users meticulously examine and modify their privacy settings on social media platforms.

Strategies for Setting and Maintaining Boundaries:

Clear Communication: The key to their effectiveness is communicating boundaries in an assertive and clear manner. Whether it is setting expectations for online interactions or expressing limitations on the kind of content one is comfortable sharing, clear communication sets the tone for respectful involvement.

Example: When a participant in an online discussion group states that the conversation should stick to the assigned topic and refrain from bringing up sensitive or personal topics, they are communicating their boundaries.

Regular Self-Assessment: Limits are dynamic; they change as people use the internet. Self-evaluation on a regular basis entails thinking back on one's online experiences, analyzing feelings, and modifying boundaries as necessary.

Example: After using social media, a user evaluates their emotional health on a regular basis. If they experience anxiety or feelings of inadequacy, they may decide to reduce the amount of time they spend on these sites or modify the amount of content they consume.

NAVIGATING SOCIAL MEDIA MINDFULLY:

Selective Content Consumption: Selecting the kind and amount of information that one interacts with on the internet is part of mindful consumption. Adding uplifting, inspirational, and informative content to one's feeds makes for a more positive and enlightening digital experience.

Example: In order to create a more encouraging and upbeat online community, users tailor their Instagram feed to feature profiles that share their values and interests.

Setting Time Limits: Setting time limits for social media use prevents excessive scrolling and makes sure that online interactions complement daily life rather than take over. Time management is essential to upholding healthy boundaries online.

Example: In order to encourage a responsible use of technology, a user makes advantage of smartphone capabilities that let users establish daily time limitations for social media apps.

ESTABLISHING PROFESSIONAL & PERSONAL BOUNDARIES:

Maintaining a Distinction: When it comes to people who use the internet for both personal and professional purposes, it is important to keep things distinct. Professional boundaries help to make sure that personal and work-related content is kept apart.

Example: A freelance writer keeps up-to-date personal and professional blogs, making sure that the content published on each platform is appropriate for the target audience and objectives.

Managing Friendships and Connections: It can be difficult to distinguish between friends, acquaintances, and professional contacts on social media. It might be helpful to manage connections carefully and be aware of the nature of online interactions in order to avoid misunderstandings or potential disputes.

Example: Social media connections are grouped by the user so they can share particular content with target audiences while still adhering to a professional demeanor.

DEALING WITH ONLINE CONFLICT:

Disengaging Constructively: Disengaging constructively means walking away from heated discussions, avoiding personal attacks, and, if necessary, seeking resolution through private communication. While online conflict is unavoidable, how people respond to it can have a big impact on their well-being.

Example: When confronted with a heated online debate, a user decides to step back for a while, stressing the value of productive discussion and indicating that they are willing to carry on in private.

Utilizing Blocking and Reporting Features: Using tools like blocking and reporting capabilities, which safe online platforms offer, to help people take control of their digital interactions is a proactive way to uphold personal boundaries in the face of harassment or inappropriate behavior.

Example: When a user is subjected to ongoing online harassment, they report the incident to the platform moderators, who then utilize the tools at their disposal to block the offending accounts and safeguard their online space.

NAVIGATING DIGITAL CONNECTIONS WITH INTENTION

A positive and fulfilling digital experience is largely attributed to safe online platforms, strategies for genuine connection-building, and the maintenance of healthy boundaries. In the vast landscape of digital connections, finding meaningful relationships requires intentional choices, mindful navigation, and the establishment of healthy boundaries.

People must approach the digital world with awareness and purpose as technology continues to change how we connect. Through utilizing safe platform features, encouraging mindfulness and authenticity in online interactions, and setting and upholding healthy boundaries, people can intentionally navigate the digital world.

The examples given show how these tactics can be used in the real world and show that when done carefully, meaningful connections can be made in the digital sphere. Whether one is looking to network professionally, find love, or form friendships based on common interests, the fundamentals of safety, authenticity, and setting boundaries still apply.

By embracing the potential for genuine connections in the digital age, people can weave a tapestry of relationships that enrich their lives and contribute to a positive and connected online community. As we continue to explore the possibilities of digital connections, it is essential to prioritize the quality of relationships over quantity and to cultivate spaces where people can engage meaningfully, free from the negative impacts of online toxicity.

8: FAMOUS STORIES OF LONELINESS

In this exploration, we delve into the lives of 20 famous personalities who have openly shared their battles with loneliness. These stories not only highlight the pervasive nature of loneliness that can affect individuals across various walks of life, but they also highlight the fact that loneliness is a universal human experience that transcends fame, wealth, and success. Celebrities often live their lives in the public eye, but their personal struggles with loneliness may not always be evident.

1. Elvis Presley (1935–1977):

Elvis Presley suffered from severe loneliness, especially in his later years, despite his famous reputation as the "King of Rock and Roll." He was alone with his problems and felt cut off from the people around him.

2. Marilyn Monroe (1926–1962):

Marilyn Monroe, the legendary Hollywood actress, suffered from mental health problems and loneliness during her glitzy career. Despite her attractive movie persona, Monroe felt alone and uneasy.

3. Michael Jackson (1958–2009):

Even with his widespread celebrity, "King of Pop" Michael Jackson struggled with self-worth, relationships, and the expectations of fame, all of which added to his deep loneliness.

4. Lady Gaga:

Despite her colorful stage persona, pop sensation Lady Gaga has been transparent about her problems with loneliness. She has talked about feeling alone in her personal life and the difficulties of sustaining real friendships.

5. Robin Williams (1951–2014):

Even though he made millions of people smile, Robin Williams, the adored comedian and actor, struggled with loneliness throughout his life, which finally led to his untimely death.

6. Selena Gomez:

Selena Gomez, an actress and pop singer, has been open about her experiences with mental health issues and loneliness. Her rise to popularity at a young age has not spared her from challenges with anxiety and sadness.

7. Kanye West:

The well-known rapper and fashion designer Kanye West coexists with a complex emotional terrain; he has been transparent about his difficulties with loneliness and the negative effects that celebrity has had on his mental health.

8. Princess Diana (1961–1997):

Princess Diana, despite being known as the "People's Princess," struggled with loneliness in the royal family's protective bubble. Her mental health issues and the demands of her public persona added to her loneliness.

9. Robert Pattinson:

The "Twilight" series star Robert Pattinson, an actor, has talked about how lonely it can be to be in the spotlight and how the intense scrutiny that comes with being famous has affected his ability to connect with people on a real level.

10. Drew Barrymore:

Drew Barrymore, an actress who gained notoriety early in life, struggled with substance abuse and loneliness. Her path to recovery and real connections emphasizes the complicated nature of celebrity.

11. J.K. Rowling:

J.K. Rowling, the wildly popular author of the "Harry Potter" series, has been candid about her struggles with depression and loneliness, especially at trying times in her life.

12. Jim Carrey:

Actor and comedian Jim Carrey is well-known for having talked openly about his experiences with loneliness, particularly during times of personal and professional upheaval. His reflective demeanor has inspired him to delve into the more profound facets of life.

13. Adele:

Adele, a Grammy-winning artist, has been open about how loneliness affected her creative process and how her grief and loneliness were the inspiration for many of her dramatic ballads.

14. Johnny Depp:

In the middle of court disputes and significant media attention, actor Johnny Depp has experienced loneliness. In addition to his captivating movie image, Depp's personal life has been characterized by difficulties that have added to his sense of loneliness.

15. Demi Lovato:

Building a supportive network has been a key component of singer and actress Demi Lovato's rehabilitation process. She has been open about her struggles with mental health concerns, including loneliness.

16. Ed Sheeran:

Ed Sheeran has openly discussed his experiences with loneliness in spite of his enormous success in the music business. The demands of touring and the solitary nature of celebrity have taken a toll on his mental well-being.

17. Winona Ryder:

Winona Ryder, an actress, has opened out about feeling lonely in spite of her success in Hollywood. Her insights on the difficulties of sustaining real relationships in the entertainment business illuminate the human side of celebrity.

18. Emma Watson:

Emma Watson, the star of "Harry Potter," has talked about her struggles with loneliness, particularly when she was a young girl managing stardom and going through periods of self-discovery.

19. Ryan Reynolds:

In his candid remarks, comedian and actor Ryan Reynolds has discussed his struggles with loneliness and anxiety, highlighting the value of building relationships and getting support.

20. Oprah Winfrey:

Despite her enormous success, media mogul Oprah Winfrey has recounted moments of loneliness .

9: CONCLUSION AND CALL TO ACTION

We sum up the journey's important lessons in the final section and exhort readers to take concrete measures toward living a more meaningful and connected life. In addition to using the suggested solutions, readers are encouraged by a call to action to forward this resource to others who might be struggling with loneliness in silence.

LESSONS LEARNED FROM BATTLING OF LONELINESS

Regardless of social standing or upbringing, everyone can learn something from these celebrities' experiences with loneliness. Here are some important takeaways from their stories:

1. Fame Does Not Equate to Fulfillment:

These celebrities' lives demonstrate that, despite receiving external validation, wealth and popularity may not always translate into inner fulfillment. Loneliness can endure even in the face of widespread acclaim.

2. Authenticity Is a Powerful Antidote:

In the fight against loneliness, embracing honesty and staying loyal to oneself seem to be effective strategies. Openly sharing personal challenges with the public has shown that vulnerability is a must for real connections.

3. Human Connection Matters Most:

These people, in spite of their notoriety, serve as a

reminder of the value of human connection. Genuine, trusting relationships are essential to preventing loneliness and promoting a feeling of community.

4. Mental Health is a Priority:

These celebrities' experiences with mental health underscore the significance of placing a high priority on mental health. Getting professional assistance, engaging in self-care, and de-stigmatizing conversations about mental health are all critical steps in the fight against loneliness.

5. Isolation in the Spotlight is Common:

Because of how isolating fame can be, a lot of celebrities experience intense loneliness. The continual focus, scrutiny, and lack of privacy can all add to a sense of isolation, underscoring the importance of support networks.

6. Success Does Not Shield from Loneliness:

Being successful in the eyes of society does not always mean that one is not lonely. These superstars show that loneliness may endure in spite of prosperity on the outside.

7. Public Image vs. Private Struggles:

Celebrities may exude confidence and contentment, but their experiences with loneliness highlight the contradiction between a public character and inner struggles. These struggles highlight the significance of realizing that everyone has personal struggles.

8. Loneliness Spans Across Generations:

Loneliness is a timeless and universal sensation that cuts across eras, affecting everyone from legendary people like Ed Sheeran and Lady Gaga to more modern luminaries like Elvis Presley and Marilyn Monroe.

9. Relationship Quality over Quantity:

Building a modest, supportive network of real connections can have a greater impact than assembling a huge, superficial social circle, demonstrating that the quality of relationships matters more than quantity.

10. Self-Reflection and Growth:

A common thread among celebrities who candidly talk about their experiences with loneliness is self-reflection and personal improvement, acknowledging the need for change, and actively pursuing personal development.

11. Navigating Transitions Can Be Challenging:

Significant changes in one's identity, profession, or relationships can all cause or worsen feelings of loneliness. It is important to acknowledge this difficulty in order to remain resilient in these circumstances.

12. Mental Health Stigma Must Be Addressed:

Recognizing and publicly addressing mental health difficulties is a step toward a more helpful culture. These celebrities' willingness to talk about their struggles with mental health helps to destigmatize the debate around mental well-being.

13. Balancing Professional and Personal Life:

Many celebrities struggle to maintain a healthy balance between their personal and professional lives. This highlights the significance of establishing boundaries and making sure that one's own needs come first.

14. Loneliness Can Coexist With External Success:

The paradoxical coexistence of loneliness within and accomplishment on the outside serves as a potent reminder that material gains and honors might not be enough to satisfy the need for connection.

15. Perceptions Can Be Deceptive:

These celebrities' experiences demonstrate how public perceptions may be misleading, with people often hiding behind attractive façades to deal with emotional troubles and loneliness.

To sum up, these celebrities' experiences with loneliness teach us that real fulfillment originates from within, based on authenticity, real connections, and putting mental health first. These lessons are applicable to people from all walks of life

10: EPILOGUE: YOUR JOURNEY BEGINS

As readers close the book, they are reminded that their journey toward connection and fulfillment is ongoing. "Beyond Solitude" isn't just a guide; it's a companion on their path towards meaningful relationships and a life rich with connection.

This book is more than a collection of words; it's a beacon of hope for those navigating the often challenging terrain of loneliness. "Beyond Solitude" is not just a book; it's a road map to a more connected, fulfilled, and enriched life.

ABOUT THE AUTHOR

The author, P K Singh, is an Electrical Engineer from Delhi College of Engineering (now Delhi Technological University) and certified Trainer from Institute of Learning & Management, UK. He is DNV, and Bureau Veritas certified ISO 9001-2015 QMS/EMS Lead Auditor having more than 40 years' experience in handling HSE, Operations, Logistics, Recruitment and Training functions in various multinational industries in India and abroad.

Within the pages of this book, the author advocates for connection; their goal is to dismantle the barriers surrounding loneliness by inviting readers to connect with them, share their stories, and create lasting bonds. By exposing the unadulterated beauty of vulnerability, they feel that we open the door to real and meaningful relationships.

Thank you

A

Book from

"pk resources"

India

www.ingramcontent.com/pod-product-compliance
Lightning Source LLC
Chambersburg PA
CBHW050742260726
48661CB00001B/372